Looking Back At

# Fair Haven

New York

A Pictorial History

Robert J. Kolsters
and
Charles H. Sweeting

BroaderBound
Publishing

*Books make unique gifts. Support history: buy a copy for a friend.*

**Looking Back at Fair Haven, New York, A Pictorial History**
by Robert J. Kolsters and Charles H. Sweeting
Copyright © 2008 by Robert J. Kolsters

First Edition

ISBN-10  0-9726841-1-5
ISBN-13  978-0-9726841-1-8

Library of Congress Control Number: 2008904055

Published in the United States of America by
Broader Bound Publishing
Post Office Box 4319
Burbank, California 91503

www.BroaderBound.Net
Publishing@BroaderBound.Net

ISBN 978-0-9726841-1-8

9 780972 684118

# To the Warriors of Preservation

This book is dedicated to those who captured the images
here within and to the keepers of these sacred treasures they
created, the determined warriors who diligently protect
this delicate evidence so it can be shared with us
and future generations who will enjoy it
for thousands of years to come.

*Blessings on each of you*
*for gently daring*
*at every turn*
*each year upon century*
*to protect what lesser hands*
*in a single, careless moment*
*might discard*
*to be lost to us - forever.*

Lord Sandefeld

Thank you for the generosity of your time, care and
attention in seeing these images survive.

# Acknowledgements

This book would not have been possible without the use of the many collections of documents and photographs so carefully preserved by so many people. Thank you for sharing your materials as well as your expertise and support.

In some cases it is impossible to guess who the photographer was that captured a particular image. Others we know for sure. To each of them we are indebted.

We have from which to choose only the photographs that have survived the journey through time - again and again, year after year, handed down to each new generation. Each of the many individual caretakers whose hands these photographs have passed through deserve praise.

Integral in getting this book completed are all those who offered suggestions, moral support, proofing and editing time. Thank you, thank you, thank you.

We would like to especially thank the follow:

| | | |
|---|---|---|
| Tay Bacon | Julie Leshay | Shirley Sinn |
| Nancy Britton | June S. MacArthur | Judy Snyder |
| Jane Sant Brockman | Phil MacArthur | Sterling Historical Society |
| Edgar Denton | Jeanettte McIntyre | Betsy Sweeting |
| Natalie Edmunds | Olive Grant Ostrander | Don Sweeting |
| John Fadden | Lezli Parsons | Hallie Sweeting |
| Fair Haven Library | Don Richardson | Heather Sweeting |
| Erwin Fineout | Raymond S. Sant | Leora Scott Van Patten |
| Lucille Flack | Raymond T. Sant | Rick Van Patten |
| Deborah Heintz | George Sheldon | Seward M. Williams |
| Linda Jackson Clum | Virginia Shepard | and, of course, |
| | | Edna E. Williams |

We sincerely apologize for overlooking anyone we've inadvertently omitted.

# Preface

## Thank you for your interest in
## Fair Haven's History

Charlie and I wished to share with you our love of Fair Haven through the images in our collections as well as photographs others have shared with us. When I started to lay out the pages for each chapter, I found I was looking at far more images than would fit within one volume. Therefore, if there is interest in this book, it will serve as the first in a series of picture books on Sterling, Fair Haven and Little Sodus Bay.

This volume focuses on images taken on or near Main Street. It is not meant to be a complete history, but simply a walk through the visual images that were available. Some things may have never been photographed and more photos, waiting in attics and basements, are yet to be seen. In some cases we trusted what was written on the back of the photo and we've added additional information if possible.

If an image in this book brings back memories or you can identify an unknown person or place, please write to me, call me, email me, or otherwise let me know. I would love to hear your stories and correct any errors only you may notice.

Please let me know if you have photographs of things that aren't here anymore or have been remodeled. Film captures detail the human eye cannot see and today's scanners and computers can reveal what is hidden in the background. Your snapshot of Uncle Fred has a clue to Fair Haven's history in the background.

Tomorrow's technologies will unveil even more we do not realize we have. What our ancestors thought was common knowledge we now wonder about. Every image is worth a thousand answers to those who were not there.

Every place has a time when its photographic history began. Though portraits were taken in studios in New York City as early as 1839, it took several years for shutters to reach every small town and village. Families and individuals certainly traveled to Auburn, Oswego, Syracuse and Rochester to have studio portraits taken before the first photographer finally lugged his glass plates to Fair Haven.

Early outdoor photography required a special lens and a photographer experienced in making natural light exposures without a modern light meter. Professional photographers were occasionally requested to make a trip from the city to photograph a new home or business. Later, photographers with their equipment traveled through the countryside looking for business and developed the images back at their labs.

Some entrepreneurs bought equipment that allowed them to develop and print photographs at home. Edna E. Williams was one Fair Havenite who studied the art of photography. Toting her tripod, she has left us with more turn of the century photographs of the area and people than any other single photographer. Eventually hand-held film cameras became available with faster shutter speeds. Anyone could make exposures, then mail the camera back to the manufacturer. The camera would be reloaded with film at the factory and sent back with the prints.

We couldn't pinpoint the date some photograph was taken. We have pointed out the photos that seem to be the earliest. The photograph of the Seth Turner House on page 72 was clearly taken more than a decade before any other we have seen. Hopefully more candidates for Fair Haven's earliest photograph will one day be found in someone's attic or basement.

These photographs help us better envision what the lives of our ancestors were like here. I am happy every will now have the opportunity to see these wonderful images. No doubt this book would have gone to press much sooner with the motivation of working regularly with Charlie until its completion. I greatly enjoyed collaborating with him and he kept us going. Nevertheless, now that I have completed it, I know Charlie would be very happy that this book is finally in your hands to enjoy.

*Rob Kolsters*

*April 24, 2008*

Post Office Box 4319
Burbank, California 91503

818-763-5800

RKolsters@DocumentedResearch.Org

# Contents

# 1853

## MAP OF
## STERLING

# Early Fair Haven

## Before The Railroads

**1857 Fair Haven** - This lithograph by George Hayward is the earliest known depiction of Fair Haven. Much of the virgin timber had long since been cleared allowing this vista from Victory Street which includes the Methodist Church, the Hunt Hotel and the smoke stack of the steam mill near Vought's Cove. At the extreme right the *Cottage Farm* cottage can been seen with its cleared view of the bay from what is now Richmond Avenue.

   The north end of Little Sodus Bay was open to Lake Ontario. Only one pier had yet been constructed to keep the channel open. The sand bar to the west would continue to naturally build up over the years.

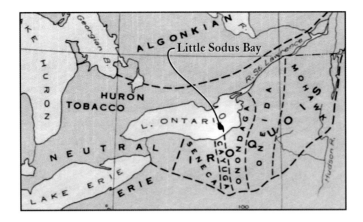

Little Sodus Bay

**1620**
**Iroquois Nations**

This map shows the area of the Five Nations of the Iroquois when few Europeans had yet visited the area.

### Date-ke-ă-o-shote

The Iroquois were familiar with Little Sodus Bay, which they called *Date-ke-ă-o-shote*. Artifacts have been found showing evidence of their hunting and fishing activities near the bay.

*Iroquois* is a term created by the French. These people referred to themselves as *Hau-de-no-sau-neeis*, meaning "The People Who Build Long Houses." For hundreds of years the Five Nations of the Iroquois lived in well constructed "long houses" in villages located in other areas of Cayuga County and throughout central New York State. No evidence has been unearthed of any permanent villages specifically in the area of Sterling prior to Europeans settling here in 1805. At that time, the Iroquois trails were known and used to traverse the township, mainly the routes of Old State Road and Sterling Station Road.

### 1776-1783 American Revolution

The Iroquois attempted to remain neutral when the colonists declared independence. The turbulent times disrupted trade Native Americans relied on and split the Nations into individual alliances. The U. S./British treaty of Versailles in 1783 held no provision protecting the Iroquois and their ancestral home. A series of treaties and land sales left the Iroquois with a few small reservations and some settled on lands in Canada, thus Iroquois activity in Sterling quickly dwindled.

**1795 Peru** - Before the township of Stirling was surveyed, the area northwest of Cato had been referred to as Peru.

In return for their service, New York's Revolutionary War soldiers were promised land. Each veteran or surviving family member received 100 acres or more, based on rank.

To fulfill this promise, an area known as the *Military Tract* was surveyed in the wilderness of central New York. This created 28 new townships consisting of 100 lots of 600 acres each.

**1802 Stirling** - Stirling was originally spelled with an *i* when it was surveyed in 1795 as the 28th and last township of the *Military Tract*.

**1804 Cayuga County Line** - Due to the shape of the shoreline, Sterling's 100 lots could not be laid out in a perfect rectangle as many of the townships were. When Seneca County was created in 1804, Sterling was split in half, the western lots going to the new county. This area is now Wayne County which was created from Seneca County in 1823.

Sterling had no permanent settlers until Pierre Dumas arrived in 1805. It was governed as part of Cato until the township of Sterling was formally organized in 1812.

Notice that this map shows the original area of Cato as it was before the townships of Victory, Ira and Conquest were created from it in 1821.

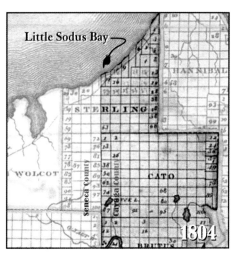

**Wildlife** - Many species that had thrived in the area for thousands of years disappeared or were deliberately eradicated soon after Europeans arrived. These are only a few of the neighbors that greeted early Fair Haven settlers.

Cougar

Wolves

Lynx

Eagle

Moose

February 18, 1894

**PLENTY OF BEARS IN NEW-YORK.**

**The State Annually Pays for Killing About 200 of Them.**

ALBANY, Feb. 18.—About 200 bears on an average are killed in New-York State annually, for the killing of which the State pays bounties. The fish and game laws provide that for every wolf killed a bounty of $30 shall be paid, for every panther $20, and for every bear $10. The conditions of receiving the bounty are that the skull of the animal shall be burned in the presence of the Game Constable and the skin branded. This is to prevent a second bounty for the same animal.

The records of claims for bounties are kept on file in the office of the Controller. Over 200 bounties for bears were paid last year, and the clerk in charge of the records estimates that the average outlay for the bears is between $2,200 and $2,500 a year.

It has been some time since bounty has been paid for killing a panther, and still longer since the last wolf bounty was paid. The banner county for bears last year was Hamilton, the number killed in that county "officially" numbering fifty-two. Essex, Saratoga, Warren, Fulton, and St. Lawrence also contributed to the list of dead. Residents of the Adirondack region say that there are a few panthers remaining, but that the wolf is probably exterminated.

Elk

Bear

**Williams Cabin**

The Roland Williams cabin near Duncan's Corners survived long enough to be photographed. Many of the first settlers in the area probably lived in homes similar to this, made from plentiful local soft woods.

Surveyors did not walk most of the boundary lines of the lots they drew on maps. The first settlers used the Iroquois trials in Sterling and branched off of these to carve out a path to their property. These ancient trails were widened into roads for wagons and we use these same routes today. None of Sterling's log cabins are known to now exist. Perhaps a log infrastructure will one day be discovered inside one of Fair Haven's modernized homes.

**Log Cabin Construction** - This is another example of a log cabin near Fair Haven built before 1830.

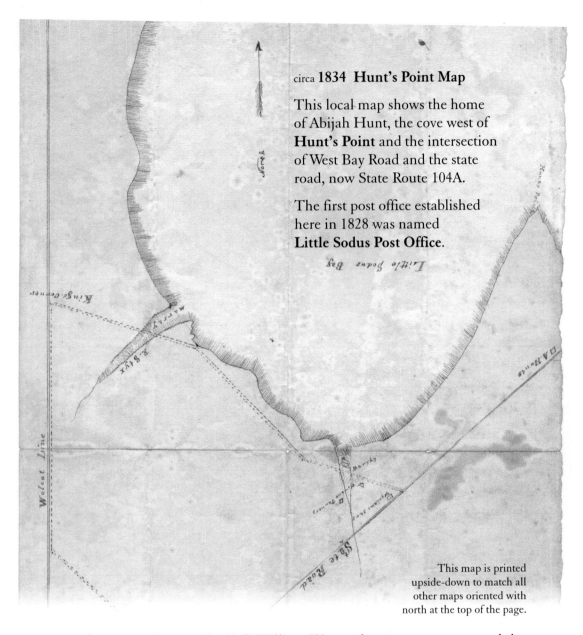

circa **1834** **Hunt's Point Map**

This local map shows the home of Abijah Hunt, the cove west of **Hunt's Point** and the intersection of West Bay Road and the state road, now State Route 104A.

The first post office established here in 1828 was named **Little Sodus Post Office**.

This map is printed upside-down to match all other maps oriented with north at the top of the page.

**Before Fair Haven** - In 1847 William Wyman became postmaster and the post office moved to his shop shown on this map. This hamlet at the head of Little Sodus Bay was known as **Little Sodus**.

Being the center of activity, the first plan for a railroad terminus called for the line to pass through this area on its way to a newly planned development named Sodusville on the north west bay shore. The final plan for the *Lake Ontario, Auburn and New York Railroad* favored the east shore and the village of Sodusville never materialized.

- This view from Turner Hill probably changed very little in the first 100 years after this land was cleared in the early 1800s.

**William Wyman's shop** ⊚ on West Bay Road housed the Little Sodus Post Office in 1847.

For over 45 years the **Hunt Hotel** ⊚ stood on the State Road, just east of where the West End Express gas station is now.

Up the hill on the south side of the road, the **Methodist Church** ⊚ commanded a prominent spot above the bay. It was moved in 1883. The roofline of the Methodist parsonage can be seen below, just over the hill on Victory Street.

circa **1928 Wyman Shop and Post Office** - This view looks northeast and shows West Bay Road as it enters from the left. The photograph was taken when the old Wyman building was still standing and after the State Road to Red Creek had been improved, about 1913.

circa **1906  Turner Hill**

Heading west, State Route 104A climbs Turner Hill after passing the turnoff onto West Bay Road on the right. In 1847 the Little Sodus Post Office was just beyond this intersection.

The first roads were not much wider than needed for two slow wagons to pass each other.  Packed dirt was sufficient for wagons, but soon automobiles were kicking up dust or causing greater ruts in the mud.

circa **1818  Early Farmhouse** - This depiction of a central New York farmhouse typifies what life was like for the first families of Fair Haven.

## circa **1810**
## **Cooper's Mill** and **Sacketsville**

This map shows Sterling after 51 of its western lots were given to Seneca County in 1804.

Sterling Center is labeled on this map as **Sacketsville** and Sterling Valley as **Coopers**.

**Cooper's Mill** was named for John Cooper, one of Sterling's first settlers and its first postmaster.

The hamlets at Little Sodus Bay and Martville were not yet large enough to be shown.

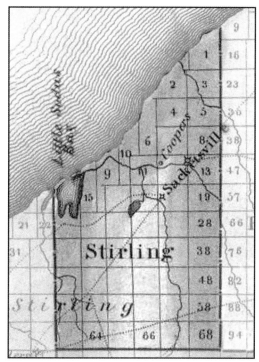

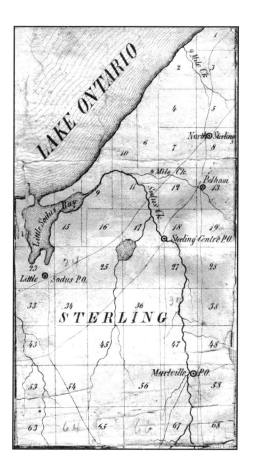

One reason place names were sometimes changed coincides with the opening of a new post office. Each post office must have a unique name within the state that is approved by the Postmaster General. Perhaps these early names were changed because they were too similar to post offices in Coopersville, Cooperstown, Coopers Plains, Sackets Harbor or one of the many other small hamlets that existed at the time.

### 1849 **Little Sodus** and **Pelham**

**Cooper's Mill** is shown as **Pelham** on this 1849 map. In 1862 the first post office here opened with the name **Sterling Valley** P. O.; Pelham P. O. in Westchester County, NY had already been established.

**Little Sodus** P. O., established in 1828, is shown at the head of the bay.

**1852  Fair Haven Gets Its Name** - Auburn mayor, Benjamin F. Hall, was one of the investors in the *Lake Ontario, Auburn and New York Railroad* who felt the word "little" was not becoming of the prosperous port they one day envisioned at Little Sodus Bay.

**Benjamin F. Hall**

In a letter to United States Postmaster General, Nathan K. Hall, he requested the name of Little Sodus Post Office be changed to Fair Haven Post Office and the bay's name impressively changed to match that of the great lake, Ontario.

Cayuga County native, President Millard Fillmore, had just appointed his lifelong friend, Nathan K. Hall, as District Court Judge for New York State.  On his last day as Postmaster General, August 31, 1852, Nathan Hall officially changed the name of Little Sodus to Fair Haven.  B. F. Hall in turn wrote to inform Fair Haven Postmaster, William Wyman, that the change had been approved.

The U. S. Postal Service had no jurisdiction over the name of the bay and thus Hall writes, "...let the bay itself be called Ontario Bay by *general consent*..."  The Customs Collector's records continued to refer to vessel activity as being at "...the port of Little Sodus."  (Later, Sandy Creek's Wigwam Cove came to be known as Ontario Bay.)

A rose
by any
other
name
would
never
smell
as sweet
as sweet
*Fair
Haven*

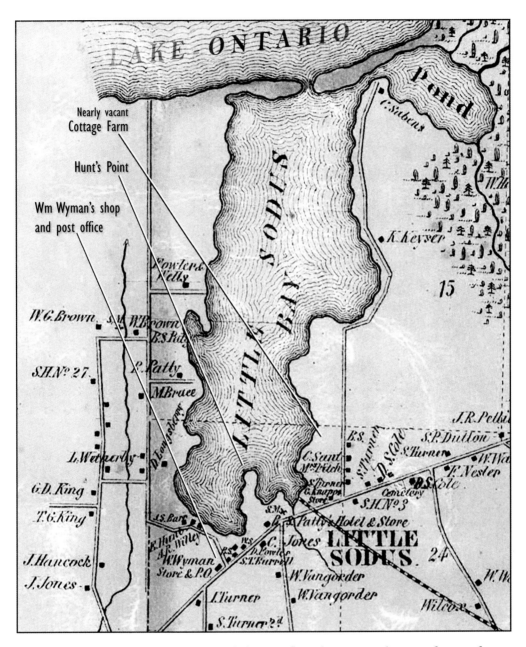

Nearly vacant
Cottage Farm

Hunt's Point

Wm Wyman's shop
and post office

**1853 Little Sodus** - This map did not reflect the recent change of name for Fair Haven. Information for the map was probably gathered well in advance of its publication the following year.

Though Fair Haven had begun to spread out, the post office was still located near West Bay Road at William Wyman's shop. Lake Street had dwellings only on its east side. The west side, to the bay, was privately held and this area on the north and south sides of Main Street would be unavailable for 20 years.

Dutch Reformed Church on Church Street    The Cottage Farm    Steam Saw Mill    Hunt Hotel    Methodist Church

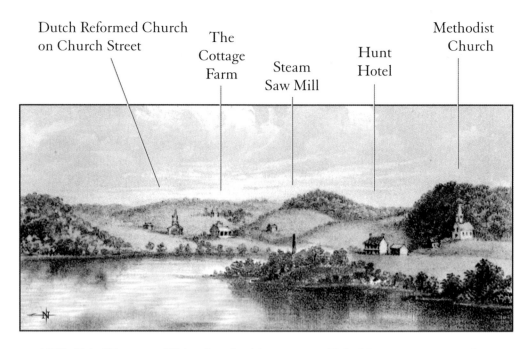

**1857 Fair Haven** - This view looking east at Fair Haven was created to promote the railway which made Little Sodus Bay a major port on Lake Ontario. Both churches can be seen in this drawing. Hunt's Point extends into the bay from the south.

circa **1857 Dutch Reformed Church**

Built in 1855, the church's cross atop the steeple stood 70 feet above Fair Haven. On December 12, 1881 a figure was seen running from the building just before it burned to the ground. This is the reason there is no longer a church on Church Street.

The congregation reorganized as the Reformed Presbyterian Church and traded this site to John Dietel for property he owned on Richmond Avenue, where they erected a new edifice.

### circa 1915 Methodist Church

The first Methodist chapel in Fair Haven was a wooden structure built in 1854 on the south side of State Route 104A across the road from where the West End Express gas station is now.

After the Methodist's brick church was completed at the corner of Main Street and Fancher Avenue in 1883, M. C. Turner moved the old church to his lot just north of the railroad depot where this photograph was taken. Turner used the building as storage for his lumber business and also operated a roller skating rink and dance hall on the large second floor.

**Methodist Parsonage** - Parsonage Street was named for this home built in 1872 at the corner of Victory Street. Its location was convenient to the church, just west across Victory Street.

Many remember Lytle and Carolyn Simons Van Patten living here. Carolyn grew up in the house.

**1857 Hunt's Point** - This lithograph of Hunt's Point and the bay is one of four created to attract investors in the planned railway to Fair Haven. In the early 1900s this became known as Eldredge Point, renamed for Frank Eldredge who purchased property here and built a summer cottage.

**Hunt Hotel** - The Hunt Hotel, at far right, featured a 40x60 foot ballroom on the third floor and immediately became a popular gathering place for social events when it was built, about 1828. The hotel had a series of owners until Giles Barrus acquired it about 1867. When Giles built a new hotel closer to the railway in 1875 he sold this structure to Charles and George Brown who dismantled it and used the lumber to build an apple dryer.

**The Cottage Farm** - At the top right we see the cottage on the *Cottage Farm* with out-buildings and its beautiful view of the bay. When Thomas Phoenix arrived from New York City with his two daughters in the summer of 1835, they rented the entire Hunt Hotel while their cottage was being built. Their 100 acre property became known as the *Cottage Farm*. This was a summer respite for "the New York ladies," as Phoenix's daughters were known, rather than a working farm.

**Kayser Point** - Phoenix's good friend, John C. Kayser of New York City, soon followed his example, purchasing the adjacent 100 acres on Kayser Point, seen here extending into the bay from the right.

**Steam Mill** - The steam sawmill on Vought's Cove, with its smoke stack had several owners, including Henry Reed.

**BUSINESS DIRECTORY**

| | |
|---|---|
| T.Harshey | Prop. of Ontario House |
| R.Patty | Prop. of Fair Haven Hotel |
| H Smith | Prop. of Lake Shore Hotel |
| T.S.Brinkerhoff | Physician & Surgeon |
| K.King | Lumber Dealer |
| D.King | Carpenter & Joiner |
| W.Lewis | Carpenter & Joiner |
| C.T.Adams | Attorney & Counsellor at Law |
| A.R.Willey | Attorney & Counsellor at Law |
| F.Kelsey J.P. | Brick Maker & Dealer in Horses |
| C.Sabins | Inspector of Customs |
| P.Denell | Mason |
| I.Wetherby | Dentist |
| C Sant | Resident |
| F.Cooper | Resident |
| J.Van Valkenburgh | Resident |

O N T A R I O   B A Y

**FAIR HAVEN**
OR
**LITTLE SODUS**

**1859 Fair Haven** - This map shows both the new name, **Fair Haven**, and the old name, **Little Sodus**. Fair Haven was later incorporated as a village in 1880. The bay is shown as **Ontario Bay**, though **Little Sodus Bay** is often still used. Ironically the bay is most frequently referred to as Fair Haven Bay though this has never been its official name.

The **Fair Haven Post Office** is shown at the Fair Haven Hotel; its owner, Robert Patty, having become postmaster in 1856.

The *proposed* course of the *Lake Ontario, Auburn and New York Railroad* is depicted on this map, running north near Lake Street. In reality this company filed bankruptcy and never reached Fair Haven. Progress was interrupted by the Civil War and the line was completed some 12 years later in 1871, as the *Southern Central Railroad* (later bought by *Lehigh Valley Railroad*).

The *Cottage Farm* property west of Lake Street remained undeveloped.

The legend at the top left lists some of those in business around the bay in 1859.

circa **1900  Hollenbeck Blacksmith Shop**

Charles Hollenbeck was one of many blacksmiths in Sterling.  Smithing was a service that handled all types of metal work including making and fixing horseshoes.

The frequency of the last name *Smith* speaks to how prevalent this occupation was long ago. Manufactured goods have replaced the need for this type of custom metal work.

**1900**
**Charles Hollenbeck**
at work in his shop.

circa **1905  William Cooper** - The occupation of a "cooper" was the craft of making casks and barrels.  William Cooper was born in 1825 and probably learned his craft from his father in a long line of coopers in the Cooper family.

circa **1905  Cooper's Cooperage** - Barrels were used to ship everything from pickles to nails in the days before cardboard boxes were mass produced.

**Van Patten Sheep** - These sheep were not always fenced-in in the early days. Clarisa Clark remembered a time when sheep roamed free on "the commons" and in and out of the *Cottage Farm* cottage before it was renovated.

**Dairy Farm** - Early cows roamed free before split rail fences and later, barbed wire. The cow constable charged fifty cents to redeem your cow from cow jail when it was found wandering about where it twernt wanted.

**Stone Fences** - Stones were plentiful in fields that needed to be cleared for planting. They were efficiently set down as fences that blocked a variety of critters from getting at the crops. Collapsed stone fences can still be seen around Sterling today.

**Nailless Fence**

Before barbed wire was invented, this type of fence could easily be constructed using the plentiful local trees without the need for nails or other hardware.

## Stacked Log Fence

This fence of stacked young trees was easy to construct and demonstrates how many trees Sterling forests had to spare.

Many people believe that our trees have dwindled to a low point today. Actually, second growth has filled many of the areas that were once clear cut.

## Byram Oxen

Gus Byram poses with his ox team. At one time there were more oxen in Sterling than horses.

Oxen are better suited for plowing and other jobs and were in use around Sterling into the 1920s.

# About Town

## Pastimes and Chores

circa **1911 Early Automobile Accident** - A classic scene of the era captured by Seward M. Williams of Martville. New to the power behind the wheel, a motorist swerves to avoid slower carriages and loses control, crashing through a farmer's fence. What expletives did the farmer and carriage drivers mutter about the dangers of the newfangled machines going too fast on narrow country roads? Has the cow, innocently leaving the roadway in the distance, escaped through the broken fence or was she the obstacle the motorist swerved to avoid?

**Wash Day** - Beryl and Jenny Deal were happy to show off their new Teachout brand washing machine, a great improvement over the old tub and washboard.

### 1914 Sally Ann Cooper

Born in 1827, "Aunt Sally" is in her late 80s in this photograph. She never tired of demonstrating the proper operation of her spinning wheel.

## Bath Time in Fair Haven

Ronnie Smith enjoys a bath on laundry day.

Ronnie was one of the founders of the Sterling Historical Society.

Laundry day was once a week, usually on Monday. Baths were usually on Saturday, and as needed.

**1933 The Architects of Life's Necessities** - For those too young to recall, this is the place you stumbled out to in the cold and dark before the miracle of modern plumbing.

### Cistern Pump

The Sant House on Victory Street once featured this pump at the kitchen sink. Water was pumped up from the cistern under the house. It was used until 1940 when the water lines were laid on Victory Street and the house was hooked up to town water.

**Fair Haven's First Telephone** - Mert and Clara Cooper demonstrate Fair Haven's first telephone. The wire originally stretched from Oscar Miller's store to the home of his son, Frank.

When Fayette Phillips was Deputy Collector of Customs for Little Sodus Bay he spent most of his time at his store on Main Street. In 1894 he had two miles of line installed between the Robinson & Phillips store to the customs office at North Fair Haven so he could be notified when ships arrived.

Residential lines for local calls and nearby towns were later provided by many small companies. Nationwide calling became available in 1928.

circa **1912 Robinson & Phillips Delivery Truck** - Irving Silliman driving the delivery truck. Notice the kerosene street lamp.

**August 1930 Barber Shop** Notice the camera and tripod in the mirror.

**1906 Bay View Home** - A guest staying at the Bay View Home mailed this postcard from Fair Haven on September 5, 1906. On the 1904 map William Stark is shown living here. This is now a private home still standing on the southeast corner of Wilcox Street and State Road 104A.

circa **1932 Little Sodus Bay** - This view from Avery Street shows the Bay View Home on Main Street. Wilcox Street is seen along the far side of this field. Notice the beautiful vegetable garden in the foreground.

Windbreak

Stove

Line Anchor

"Ice Spud"
to chore the hole

## Ice Fishermen

Ice fishing in the middle of the bay was a popular winter pastime.

The day had warmed up enough for John Follett, Harold Williams and Bob MacArthur to remove their jackets. But, still no fish?

**Fishing** - A crowd gathers around a large catch of sturgeon.

# STERLING.

The post office addresses of the residents of this town are *Fair Haven*, *Martville*, *North Sterling*, *Sterling* and *Sterling Valley*, in the town; *North Victory*, in the town of Victory, and *Red Creek*, Wayne County.

## FAIR HAVEN.

Barrus, Giles, prop'r Ontario House and farmer leases 130.
BARTHOLF, BENJ. A. REV., pastor Reformed Prot stant Dutch church.
BRUNDAGE, BENJ. V., painter, wagon maker and farmer 3.
Carman, Stephen H., farmer 89.
CLAPER, JACOB, farmer leases 120.
CLARK, WM. H., wagon maker.
Cochrane, James T., farmer 15½.
Cole, D. S., farmer 4 and leases 112.
Cole, Geo., farmer 106.
Crane, Henry, farmer 49.
Crane, Sherborne H., shoemaker, tanner and postmaster.
Demill, Philip, stone mason and farmer 1.
Farnham, A. J., farmer 92½.
Forscutt, John, farmer 175.
Hammond D., farmer leases 106.
Harris, John, (*with Mrs. Sarah and Mrs. J.,*) farmer 103.
Harris, J. Mrs., (*with Mrs. Sarah and John,*) farmer 103.
Harris, Sarah Mrs., (*with Mrs. J. and John,*) farmer 103.

Heislar, Frederick, farmer 49.
Jones, A. Mrs., farmer 1.
LITTLE, LUDO B., saw mill stave factory and farmer 20.
Martin, John, farmer leases from A. Bardsley, of Auburn, 140.
McCrea, John, farmer 196.
PETITT, DORASTUS, farmer 35.
Pettit, Jonathan R., farmer 70.
POST, GEO. I., lawyer and farmer 140.
Rasbeck, J. C., farmer 58.
ROSE, JAS. E., cabinet maker.
Taylor, Garrison, grocer.
TAYLOR, HENRY, sailor.
Turner, Betsy Mrs., farmer 17.
Turner, Geo., farmer 140.
Turner, Isaac Jr., farmer 60.
Turner, Wm. C., farmer 110.
VanPetten, Minard, allo. physician.
Wake, Jos., farmer 1½.
Welch, Rufus S., general merchant and farmer 5.
WILKINSON, PHILASTER, farmer 4.
Williams, John, farmer 43.
WYMAN, SIDNEY I., dep. collector of customs and farmer 23.

**1868 Business Directory of Fair Haven** - This directory listed only some of the businesses in Fair Haven.

circa **1920**
**Fair Haven Citizens Band**

The band plays from the back of Roy Rasbeck's truck.

# Main Street

## A Walk Down The North Side

**July 4, 1923  Downtown Fair Haven**  -  Today, Main Street is also known as State Route 104A and is part of the *Seaway Trail*, the scenic connection between Lake Ontario shore destinations.  A few old maps show this as Genesee Street, the name of the main street in many central and western New York towns.

**1904 Map of Fair Haven** - This book contains pictures of some of the homes and businesses shown on this 1904 map. It also contains pictures of buildings that were gone before this map was made and some that were built after this map was made. Many places changed ownership from the names shown on the map.

**Hunt's Point** - Hunt's Point eventually became known as Eldredge Point, after Frank Eldredge purchased a large portion of the point property.

In 1904, the old Hunt Hotel has been gone nearly thirty years.

In 1904, William Wyman's shop is still here, but the post office has moved to Mendel's store in the brick block.

In 1904, the old Methodist church building is gone. It has been moved over near Lake Street.

The Methodist's first parsonage is still on Victory Street.

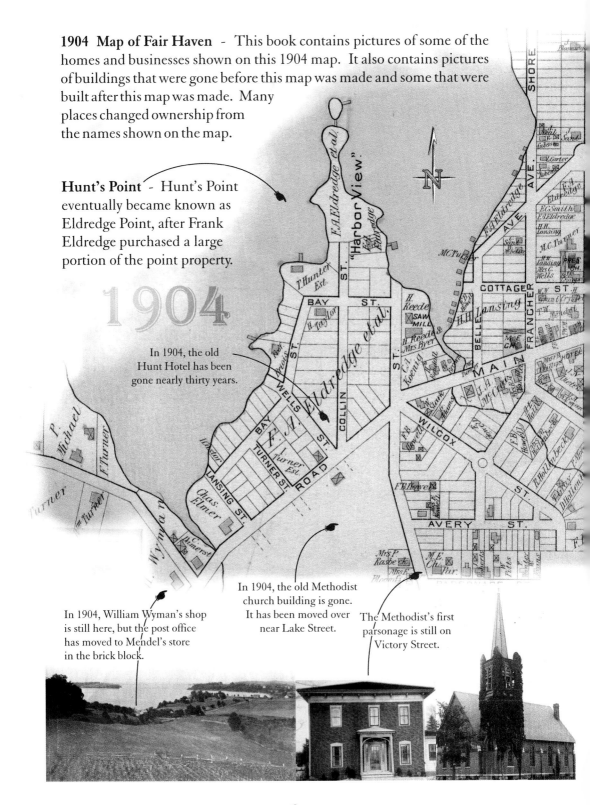

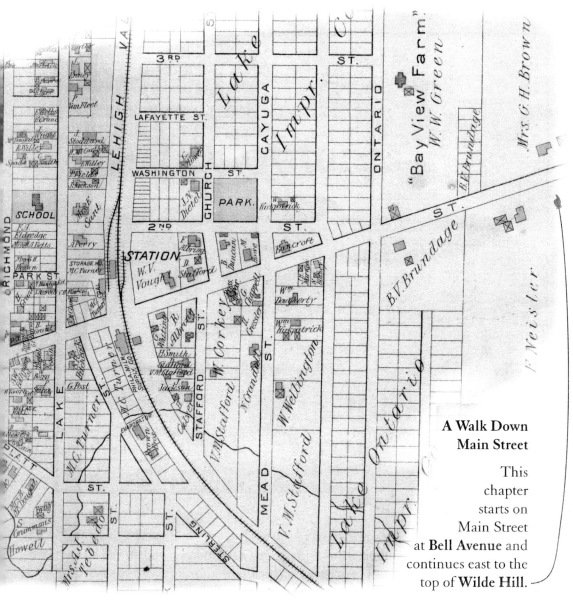

## A Walk Down Main Street

This chapter starts on Main Street at **Bell Avenue** and continues east to the top of **Wilde Hill.**

Chapter 4 returns down the south side of Main Street, back to Bell Avenue (shown as Bell*e* Avenue on this map). You can recognize where the railroad tracks once crossed Main Street near Screwy Louie's because the railway bed is now part of the County Parks system. A sign marks the trail.

circa **1914 Methodist Parsonage** - This parsonage next door to the Methodist Church on Main Street between Bell and Fancher Avenues was built in 1914 by Charles Griggs. This replaced the previous parsonage on Victory Street.

**July 4, 2003 Main Street** - Though the church is gone, this former Methodist parsonage is still a residence hidden behind these now grown trees.

circa **1915 Methodist Church** - This church once stood at the northwest corner of Fancher Avenue and Main Street. It was completed in 1883 by Joseph Bloomingdale using locally made brick.

circa **1922 Reverend Arthur T. Clark**

Reverend Clark stands in front of the Methodist Church building after he had successfully helped to merge Fair Haven's Methodist and Presbyterian congregations. The two became **Fair Haven Federated Church** in 1922. The steeple of the Presbyterian Church on Richmond Avenue can be seen on the right in the background. Both buildings were maintained for a few years, the Methodist building having heat during colder months. When the boiler blew up it prompted a decision to give up the cost of one of the locations.

After serving as a pilot during World War I, Reverend Clark continued to fly and became known as "The Flying Pastor" of Fair Haven.

### circa **1903 Methodist Church**

The north west corner of Main Street at Fancher Avenue is now empty.

### **1934 Methodist Church**

When the Federated Church voted to give up this location in favor of using the Presbyterian chapel, the community wished to see this sturdy brick building put to good use as a public meeting hall, but could not raise the three

thousand dollar asking price set by the regional Methodist authorities. The church was dismantled in 1934 and sold for scrap. Local men purchased and preserved the front doors as well as some of the stone and stained-glass windows in constructing the small chapel at Springbrook Cemetery.

**Tennis Court** - A tennis court with a view of the bay was once maintained behind the Methodist Church on Fancher Avenue.

circa **1894 Spaulding Block** - These three buildings were built at different times and each one was known as "a block." The store on the left was the Spaulding Block built in 1884 for O. F. Miller's store. Later it was Farnsworth's Cash Store and then Griggs Grocery. Fancher Avenue intersects Main Street between this store and the Methodist Church.

Robinson & Phillips Block on the right has a fine selection of sleds and snow shovels on display out front though there is yet little snow on the ground. All of these buildings are now gone and Bayside Grocery is located here.

**1915 Mr. Lydel** and **Osgar Elmer**
in front of **Charles H. Griggs Grocery**

circa **1910**
### Farnsworth's Cash Store

The photograph at the top right was taken after this became the Charles H. Griggs Grocery in 1914.

Next door, on the roof of Frank Howell's store, is a triangular framework that held Fair Haven's unique fire bell. To sound the alarm, someone would climb the ladder to the roof and bang on a metal ring with a hammer.

The early wooden boardwalks have been replaced with concrete by this time.

circa **1890  Brown's Furniture
    and Undertaking Parlor**

Known as Lyon's Block, this furniture and
casket store, with its wooden boardwalk, was
built by George Lyon in 1883 at a cost of $2,500.

George then sold the business to G. H. Brown
who sold out to Frank B. Howell in 1898.
Frank sold furniture and caskets and served as
Fair Haven's undertaker.  The first telephone
switchboard was located here.

In the 1920s Frank turned his store into the
Lakeside Theatre, showing silent films.

PICTURES
PAR EXCELLENCE

Lakeside  Theatre

F. B. HOWELL
Owner & Manager

45

**1896 Robinson & Phillips Store** - Standing on the wooden boardwalk are **E. R. Robinson**, **Irving Silliman**, clerk, and **Fayette B. Phillips**. Seated in the sailor suits are **Walter** and **Carl Phillips**. **Oscar Vought** mans the delivery wagon. Robinson & MacArthur had started the business in the Mendel Block next door. When Fayette B. Phillips bought out MacArthur's interest in 1881 they had this new building erected.

The street lamp on the post is an example of the oil (later kerosene) lamps used to light Fair Haven's streets for many years before electric street lights were installed in 1921. Each evening the lamplighter would carry his footstool and oilcan through the streets, individually lighting each lamp.

The door at the right lead upstairs to the medical office of Dr. George S. Post.

E. R. Robinson

circa **1896 Robinson & Phillips Store** - **Fayette B. Phillips, E. R. Robinson, Irving Silliman** and **Oscar Vought** ready for customers. In the days before travel was easy on smooth roads in automobiles, general stores had to carry a great variety of items local shoppers might only occasionally need. The center rack contains packets of seeds.

Fayette B. Phillips was one of Fair Haven's mayors.

Fayette B. Phillips

circa **1923**
**Christmas Displays**

Children and adults looked forward to seeing the lavish decorations and assortment of gifts the store stocked at Christmas time.

STATEMENT.

Fair Haven, N. Y., _Feb 7_ 1893

M Jenn Sterley for J Hollenbeck

To **Robinson & Phillips,** Dr.,

DEALERS IN

**GENERAL MERCHANDISE.**

| 1892 | | | | |
|---|---|---|---|---|
| Dec | 21 | 1 Flour ¹²⁰ 5 ¾ Pork ⁵⁸ chew ¹⁰ | 1 | 88 |
| 1893 | | | | |
| Jan | 4 | 2 Soap ¹⁰ Starch ⁵ Prussian Blue ⁵ | | 20 |
| " | 5 | Pepper ¹⁰ 3 ½ Shirting ³⁵ 1 oil ⁸ | | 53 |
| " | 7 | 1 ¾ Butter ⁴⁰ 2 Lard ²⁵ 4 ½ Pork ⁵⁶ | 1 | 21 |
| " | 13 | Just oil ⁵ 2 bread ¹⁰ 2 Sugar ¹⁰ | | 30 |
| | | 2 ⁶ Butter ⁵² 2 Soap ¹⁰ Muttens ³⁰ | | 92 |
| " | 20 | nutmeg ² oil ⁵ 2 Sugar ¹⁰ | | 17 |
| " | 23 | ½ Flour ⁵⁵ starch ¹⁰ bread ⁴ Graham ²⁵ | | 94 |
| " | 27 | ½ oil ⁴ 3 qt Molass ⁴⁵ | | 49 |
| " | 31 | 2 ½ Pork ³⁸ chew ¹⁰ yeast ⁵ | | 53 |
| Feb | 4 | 3 ½ Pork ⁵³ ½ oil ⁴ Salt ⁵ Flour ⁵⁵ 2 chimneys ¹⁰ | 1 | 27 |
| | | | $8 | 74 |

Recd Payment

Robinson + Phillips

48

circa **1922 Phillips & Silliman Store** - **Iva B. Phillips Vought** (daughter of Fayette Phillips), **Fayette B. Phillips** and **Irving A. Silliman**. Irving became a partner in the store in 1912 when Robinson retired.

**1941 Phillips & Silliman Store** - Irving Silliman had worked at the store for more than 60 years when he retired and handed the key to Earl Houghtaling.

circa **1948  Red & White Store**

The Phillips & Silliman store became the Red & White
store in 1941.

**1955  Fire**

Fire broke out just after midnight on
March 18, 1955 destroying all three of the wooden structures.

circa **1925 Main Street** - The bus on the left, parked in front of the post office at Mendel's, was used to bring visitors from Sterling Station to the Maplewood Inn on the right. Today, the site of the Inn is the Village Park at Richmond Ave.

circa **1920 Post Office** - The Mendel Block was also known as the Brick Block. The post office was located in Mendel's store from 1889 until 1934. Taber Mendel and his son, Leslie, served as postmasters during 35 of these years.

circa **1881 Mendel Block** - Mendel and Hitchcock built this brick block in 1876, containing three stores. The Robinson & MacArthur store opened here. Fayette Phillips bought out MacArthur's share in 1881. In 1883 Robinson & Phillips moved to their new building next door. This is now the parking lot in front of the Bayside Ice Cream stand. The photographer is standing in front of Barrus House, the hotel that became the Maplewood Inn.

Taber W. Mendel

Sometimes it is difficult to locate the exact date a building was constructed. In this case, the following newspaper item indicates that the mortar used in setting the brick for this building was fresh on September 15, 1876.

September 15, 1876

—People who are out evenings, driving their fast nags on main street, should take into consideration that the walls of the brick block are green, and rapid driving creates a jar that will prove very disastrous to the structure.

circa **1910  Mendel's Store**  -  Mendel was known for the many styles of shoes he carried as well as a vast assortment of other items to choose from.

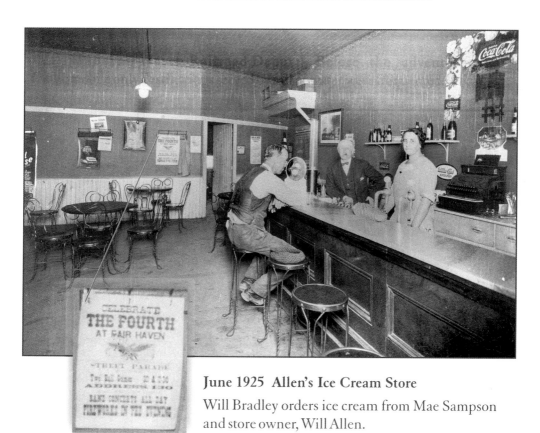

**June 1925  Allen's Ice Cream Store**
Will Bradley orders ice cream from Mae Sampson and store owner, Will Allen.

**Central Hall** - The second floor of Mendel's brick block was known as Central Hall and was used for dances, plays, lectures, meetings, demonstrations by traveling snake oil salesmen and as a schoolroom when the need arose.

circa **1890 Mendel House** - Leslie, Taber and Mary Mendel. Taber Mendel's home, directly behind his business block, on Richmond Avenue is easily seen from Main Street now that the store is gone.

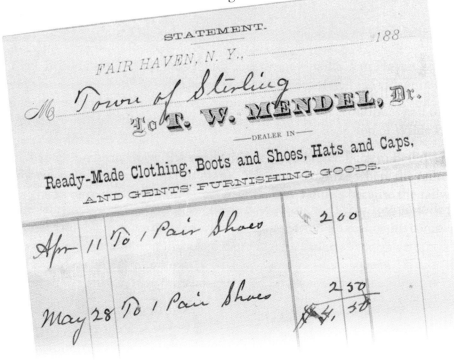

STATEMENT.

FAIR HAVEN, N. Y., _____ 188_

M _Town of Sterling_

To **T. W. MENDEL, Dr.**

—DEALER IN—

Ready-Made Clothing, Boots and Shoes, Hats and Caps,

AND GENTS' FURNISHING GOODS.

| | | |
|---|---|---|
| Apr 11 | To 1 Pair Shoes | $2.00 |
| May 28 | To 1 Pair Shoes | 2.50 |
| | | $4.50 |

circa **1950 Brick Block** - By the 1950s this building was in bad condition. There had been a fire on the second floor.

**Controlled Burn** - Harold Wallace purchased the Mendel Block and had the fire department conduct a controlled burn, then pushed the building down. The property was used to expand the size of the parking lot for Wallace's grocery store next door which is now Bay View Grocery.

Robinson & Phillips   Mendel's Brick Block   Later, MacArthur's Grocery   Now, Cutters Inn

**1908 Dean's Boots and Shoes** - The building at the far right, now Cutters Inn, was Dean's Boots and Shoes. Civil War veterans once held G.A.R. meetings upstairs. In 1926 Fair Haven National Bank opened in this building.

circa **1910 MacArthur's Grocery** - Now gone, this building on the northeast corner of Main Street and Richmond Ave. later became MacArthur's Grocery.

circa **1954 Savannah Bank Location** - At the far left can be seen the edge of the Cutters Inn building which was once Fair Haven National Bank. The 1950 Ford in the foreground, the 1954 Buick and 1948 Pontiac across the street suggest that this photo was taken about 1954.

**2003 Savannah Bank** - Today, the location in the top photo is Savannah Bank at 598 Main Street. This was taken during the 4th of July parade, 2003.

circa **1952  Fair Haven Register** – The lettering on the awning of the small building on the right reads, "The Register."  The Register was published in Fair Haven for decades.  After a few changes in name it was consolidated into the Wayuga Press Post-Herald in 1992.  The building has hosted a number of businesses over the years, including Rich Netli's shoe repair.

**2003  Bradley Building** - The building at the right was built by William Bradley, replacing Herb Grant's building that had burned at this location.

**1940 Water Lines** - Laying of water lines began in 1940 and took several months to complete. The Village provided that all work went to local men with families to support. At the far left, on the south side of Main Street, we can see Doc Hanford's office before the front porch was enclosed.

**1971 The Woodshed**

Merton Cooper, Matt Osterhoudt and Reverend Arthur T. Clark in front of The Woodshed on Main Street west of Lake Street.

This building had been the office of the *Fair Haven Register*.

circa **1928  Main Street** - The sign at the near left reads, "W. S. MacArthur People's Grocery and Meat Market."  Further down the same side of the street is the sign for "Bradley's Grocery and Meat Market."

**1969**
**Polaris Snowmobiles**

Formerly the *Fair Haven Register* office, Polaris later became The Woodshed.

**Gene's Hair Fashions**

The beauty shop was always busiest just before prom night.

This was formerly Bradley's meat market built in 1908.

**Family Restaurant** - Also remembered as the Sub-shop, the Family Restaurant building looks the same now even though it is no longer in business.

circa **1907  Grant Block** - The previous building at this location burned in 1884.  Herb Grant later built the store seen here.  About 1901 the Longley's Market portion of the building was added on the left.

circa **1907** **Longley's Market** and **Clark's Confectionary** - Lake Street runs north from Main Street between these two buildings. Herb Grant owned the building on the left and his storefront is seen just to the right of Longley's Market. On January 1, 1908 G. H. Lindsley took over Longley's Market to open his meet market here. In March of that year the building was lost to fire.

In April Herb Grant purchased F. M. Clark's confectionary across Lake Street. Mr. Clark then invested his money in building the Pleasant Beach Hotel. The tall flag pole in front of the confectionary was installed by Mr. Clark in 1896 for the McKinley election.

circa **1944**
**Bradley Building**

After Lindsley's Meat Market burned in 1908, Will Bradley built his meat market at the same location.

By the time this photo was taken, Bradley was no longer in business. But, this building is still here today.

**Grant's Soda Parlor**  -   Herb Grant bought Clark's confectionary in 1908 and was in business here for thirty years.

circa **1912  Grant's Pool Room**  -   Allen and Herb Grant playing pool.

**Grant's Soda Parlor** before and after remodeling.

circa **1912 Grant's Soda Parlor** - The wall has been opened to the back room.

**1915 Suffragettes Float** - The sign atop this 1915 float in the Fourth of July parade reads, "Rights for Women." The horses have paused in front of Herb Grant's soda parlor which is now Holdridge Realty.

**1919 Temperance Wagon** - The Fair Haven Women's Christian Temperance Union (WCTU) rode on this entry in the Fourth of July parade, campaigning against the evils of ardent spirits. Eventually their efforts were successful in helping to pass the 18th amendment to the U. S. Constitution. Prohibition began in 1920 and ended in 1933. This picture was taken in front of Herb Grant's soda parlor.

circa **1946 Food Haven** - Harriet and Jake Longley took over Grant's soda parlor in 1938, renaming it Food Haven. They give it this face lift in 1940 before selling out to John Joynt in 1946. In 1953 Mary and Michael Lombardo purchased it from John Joynt.

circa **1946 Food Haven** - Who is this ice skater? One of the Longely girls?

circa **1903 Wilde Hill** - The railroad crossing sign indicates where the railroad tracks cross Main Street on the west side of Wilde Hill. The Fair Haven depot is just out of sight on the left.

circa **1912 Fair Haven Depot** - Talk of a railroad started as early as 1851, but the first train did not reach Fair Haven until 1871. This engine arrived at the Fair Haven depot from North Fair Haven and is now headed to Auburn. On the right is the Griggs & McCrea Evaporator.

circa **1910  Fair Haven Railroad Depot** - Before the advent of the automobile only destinations served by rail or water were frequented.

**Fair Haven Depot** - Ball players practice throwing in front of the Fair Haven depot on the north side of Main Street. Perhaps they're warming up while waiting to catch a train to bring them to a game.

## Roller Rink

This building was originally the Methodist Church. In 1883, after the new brick church was completed, M. C. Turner moved this building to a lot just north of the railway depot. Turner used it as storage for his lumber business and also operated a roller skating rink and dance hall on the large second floor.

**1953 Last Train** - Lehigh Valley engine 218 leaves Fair Haven station for the last time. This trip completed Lehigh Valley's contract to deliver coal for the Turner brothers. Passenger service had already been discontinued.

**1956 Timco Office** - Timco's office building was completed in 1956 just east of the old railroad bed on land sold by Lehigh Valley. They processed canned tomatoes as well as dog and cat food in buildings behind this office. This building's colors matched their labels.

circa **1955**
**Timco Billboard**

This unique round billboard stood on Main Street just east of the Timco office.

circa **1845 Seth Turner House** - This is one of the oldest homes in Fair Haven and this may be the oldest surviving photograph taken in Fair Haven. Seth Turner hired David King to build this home in the 1840s or earlier.

The boy on the porch is said to be Seth's son, Edward, as described on the back of the photograph. Edward was born in 1828. Even if he were small for his age, this would date the photograph in the early 1840s.

The photograph appears to be a daguerreotype. Outdoor daguerreotypes are rare. Most photographs from the 1840s are indoor portraits where subjects could sit perfectly still for the long exposure time required. (This is why people in old pictures are never smiling. It was difficult to hold still with a grin.)

Ambrotypes were introduced in the early 1850s. If this photograph is an ambrotype, it could not have been taken in the 1840s and the boy is certainly too small to be Edward. Regardless, both photographic processes place this image before 1860, the year Seth Turner died. No other photograph from this time period is known to exist of Fair Haven.

Surprisingly, the railroad investors wishing to portray Fair Haven's potential brought a lithographer with them to produce the drawings of their 1857 visit, rather than a photographer. Seth Turner could afford to have paid a premium for this photographer to travel to Fair Haven from the city. Hopefully he took other photographs in Fair Haven on this day which will one day turn up.

**2003 Seth Turner House** - Seth Turner's home still stands on Main Street at the corner of Church Street.

### Naomi Brown

Seth Turner was the first postmaster for Little Sodus, serving from 1828 to 1847.

One hundred years later in 1947, his great-granddaughter, Naomi Brown, became postmistress for Fair Haven. She also lived in this house.

**View from Wilde Hill** - Looking west from her home on Ontario Street, Edna Williams captured her view of Fair Haven which extended across the bay, beyond West Bay Road and into Wayne County.  No wonder her home was ·
known as
*Bay View Farm*.

### Edna E. Williams

Edna learned to develop her own photographs at home using glass negatives. Many were reproduced as popular postcards.

Some of the images in this book are known to have been taken by Edna Williams.  Many others are probably hers.  For example, is this a self-portrait or did someone else click the shutter?

# Main Street

## A Walk On The South Side

circa **1908 Wilde Hill** - Looking east toward Juniper Hill from the top of Wilde Hill, Charles Wilde's home is seen on the right.

Today this is State Route 104A. Clearing roads on days like this was hard physical work. Good thing room for one buggy was all that was needed in those days. The road was not much wider than this on snowless days.

circa **1930  Cole House** - Built about 1829 for Darius Cole, this house is on Main Street opposite Ontario Street.  The stepped roofline has since been removed and this is now a group home.

circa **1940 Dutch Reformed Church Manse** -  This is one of the few brick homes in Fair Haven.  It was built from locally made brick as the manse for

the Dutch Reform-
ed Church,
sometime after the
church was built in
1855.  It was
conveniently
located one block
from the church for
which Church
Street is named.

After the church
burned in 1881, this
manse was given
up in favor of a
home purchased on
Richmond Avenue
next door to the
new church.

circa **1993**
**Stafford House**

John Clark's blacksmith and carriage shop was once located in the barn behind this house. Here John Clark created the large threaded bolts used to hold together cribbing in construction of the piers that keep the channel open to Lake Ontario.

Calvary Baptist Church purchased this house in 1965 for use as Bible Study rooms. In 1971 it was remodeled as the parsonage for Reverend Daryl M. Butler. The house is located on the south side of Main Street, just east of the church.

**Calvary Baptist Church** - The Calvary Baptist Church is on the south east corner of Main Street and Meade Street.

**1965 Wilkinson Dairy** - Before 1847, a school house and cemetery were located here. Baggs Feed Mill burned here in 1933. This is now the parking area west of Screwy Louie's sporting goods store.

circa **1894 Milk Station** - The Dairy Dispatch milk-house was built in 1894 along the west side of the tracks. Milk from local farms was loaded into refrigerated railcars for shipment. Main Street crosses the tracks in the foreground.

circa **1918 Milk Station** - Beyond the milk station in the distance is Baggs Feed Mill. This is the only picture of Baggs Feed Mill we have found. Do you have one? At the far right is Hayward's store before the brick was added and to its left is the foundation for the Independent Order of Odd Fellows (IOOF) which sat uncompleted from 1917 to 1924.

circa **1930 Traffic Light** - Anna Taber in front of *The Register* office, having become its editor in 1927. Notice Fair Haven's only traffic light at Lake Street when this was the main route to Fair Haven Beach State Park.

 circa **1948 Firehouse** - This was Fair Haven's second firehouse. Fire fighting changed quite a bit when fire hydrants were installed in 1940-41.

circa **1924 IOOF Hall In Winter** - The IOOF hall was completed in 1924. It was designed by Wells Bennett and constructed by Albert Baggs. Notice the electric street light.

**1968 Knick-Knacks** - The IOOF building has been saved and completely remodeled as Saint Jude's Catholic Church. Knick-Knacks souvenier shop is now Fair Haven Gift Shop. It was originally a Good Year Service Station.

**Saint Jude's Church** - Stained glass windows were added when the IOOF was remodeled for Saint Jude services.

**Good Year Service Station** - A horse and buggy were often still seen, but the writing was on the wall.

**2003 Fair Haven Gift Shop** - This building once housed the Fair Haven Fire Department.

**2003
Hayward's Grocery**

Now on Main Street, on the south east corner at Lake Street, it is said that Fred Hayward moved this building here from the gully near Vought's Creek. The brick was added later.

circa **1942  Miner House**

Mrs. Miner's house can be seen on the left.  She sold antiques here.

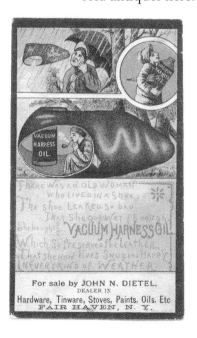

**Dietel Hardware**

On the right is Dietel Hardware.

circa **1876  Dietel Hardware Store** - John N. Dietel opened this hardware store in 1875.  This is one of the early photographs taken in Fair Haven, possibly taken when the store first opened.  Notice the hitching posts.

**2003  Dietel Hardware Store** -  Fair Haven's oldest store.  After more than 100 years as a hardware store, it became an antique store.

circa **1920  Dietel Hardware Store**  -  **Charlie Dietel** continued to operate the family business after his father, John N. Dietel, passed away in 1920.  Notice the full line of brand new cast iron stoves. Gas and electricity did not reach Fair Haven homes until later.

JOHN. N. DIETEL,
DEALER IN
**Hardware,**
**STOVES, &**
**Tinware.**
CROCKERY, GLASS
WARE, WOOD &
WILLOW-WARE.
*Tin Roofing, and Spouting, a Specialty.*
Fair Haben, N. Y.

### John N. Dietel

Born in Germany in 1849, he came to America with his parents in 1863 at the age of 14.

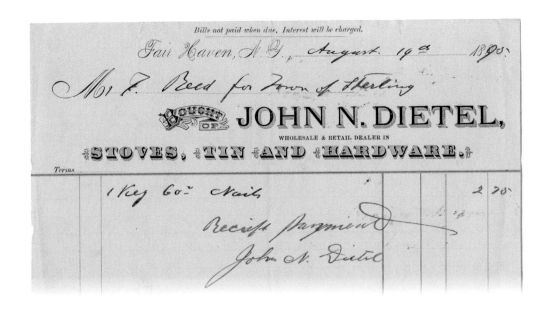

circa **1876  Dietel Hardware**  -  John N. Dietel in front of his store.

circa **1956**
**R. D. Smith
Hardware**

Ronnie Smith in
front of his store.

circa **1960  R. D. Smith Hardware**

Ronnie Smith was the great-grandson of John N. Dietel.  He purchased the store from his uncle, William Dietel, in 1950 an renamed it R. D. Smith Hardware.

**Ronnie Smith**

Ronnie was one of the founders of the Sterling Historical Society.

**2003 Doctor's Office** - Once the home and office of Doctor Virginia McKnight and other later Fair Haven physicians - in 1998 this became the Curious Moon café and gift shop.

### Dr. Virginia McKnight

Born Virginia Harley in Lima, Ohio, she married Dr. George McKnight. In 1918 she was appointed President of the village of Fair Haven to fill a vacancy in that office, making her one of the first female mayors in the country. The following year she was elected to a full term. Her niece, Dr. Eva McKnight, also became a physician.

circa **1905  First Gas Pump** - This is the first pump in Fair Haven where motorists could purchase petrol for their newfangled horseless carriages after deciding against buying a new horse. Across the street is Hotel Dietel.

circa **1919  Main Street Crowd** - Without radio or television, getting late breaking news was a community event. Here a crowd spills into the street outside the Fair Haven Register office awaiting election outcome, fight results, or other important news of the time - perhaps *The Great War* ended on this day.

**1969 Veterans Memorial** - The village park on the southwest corner of Main Street and Richmond Avenue was once the site of the Barrus House hotel. Kenneth McGuire, Wesley Van Graafeiland, Charles Wilkinson and Donald King pose in front of this memorial for Sterling's veterans after it was moved here from the corner of Lake Street.

**1969 Liquor Store**

The southeast corner of Main Street and Richmond Avenue.

At one time Fair Haven's telephone switchboard was located here before this became the

newspaper offices for The Fair Haven Register. Now it is Hair Haven.

circa **1875 Barrus House** - The *Cottage Farm* extended from Lake Street to the bay. New York City Investors had purchased the *Cottage Farm* property well in advance of the arrival of the railroad in anticipation of property values rising once trains began rolled into Fair Haven. They arrived in 1871.

In 1874 the *Cottage Farm* was surveyed into lots and sold. Fair Haven businessmen began buying lots along Main Street to build on. Giles C. Barrus quickly secured lot 146 at the corner of Richmond Avenue, much closer to the railroad depot than the old Hunt Hotel he owned on Hunt's Point.

His new hotel opened the following summer in 1875. When Giles died two years later his sons, Oscar and Giles F. Barrus, took over management of Barrus House.

## BARRUS HOUSE,

### AN ATTRCTIVE SUMMER RESORT

Beautifully located at Head of Fair Haven Bay. Is surrounded by shade trees, and has a balcouy on the front from which a splendid view of the harbor and surrounding country can be obtained

A Croquet Ground is connected, and has all modern implements for the game. Also Play Grounds for children entirely free from danger.

## A LIVERY STABLE

Is connected and good stylish rigs, and gentle horses for ladies to drive are furnished at any time. Beautiful **Row** and **Sail Boats** are always at hand, fishing tackle and everything furnished that is required for comfort or pleasure.

*The rooms are large, well furnished, & Airy.*

## THE TABLES

Are filled with all the delicasies of the season, rendering this house every way attractive to people who wish to spend a few days or the season. Mr. Barrus the proprietor, has spent almost a lifetime in keeping Hotels, and caters to please his guests.

Charges very reasonable. Terms of board can be had on application.

☞ People who want a nice quiet place, free from noise or dust, with good meals, and good society, should try the Barrus House.

circa **1895 Hotel Dietel** - John Dietel purchased the hotel in the 1890s. This picture shows the full width of Main Street from sidewalk to sidewalk. Notice the carriage stoop.

**1907 Hotel Dietel** - Edna Williams created many "real photo" postcards from her original negatives. Possibly taken earlier, this one is postmarked 1907.

**1910  Allen Inn Lounge** - W. I. Allen poses in the hotel lounge where guests could compose a letter, read or play the piano.  Optometrists, insurance agents and other businessmen visited monthly and used the hotel to meet with clients.

**1910 Allen Inn Lobby** - W. I. Allen managed Hotel Dietel before purchasing the hotel from Dietel in 1910.  Notice the convenient spittoon.

circa **1910  The Allen Inn**

Long time manager of
the Hotel Dietel,
Will Allen, bought the
hotel from John Dietel in
1910 and changed the
name to The Allen Inn.

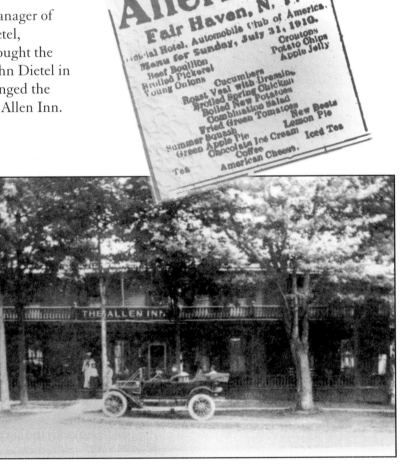

**Allen Inn**
Fair Haven, N. Y.
...ficial Hotel, Automobile Club of America.
Menu for Sunday, July 31, 1910.
Beef Bouillon                         Croutons
Broiled Pickerel              Potato Chips
Young Onions                  Apple Jelly
Roast Veal with Dressing
Broiled Spring Chicken
Boiled New Potatoes
Combination Salad
Fried Green Tomatoes            New Beets
Summer Squash              Lemon Pie
Green Apple Pie
Chocolate Ice Cream    Iced Tea
Coffee
Tea        American Cheese.

circa **1925  Maplewood Inn** - Those who owned automobiles drove from far and wide to enjoy the Inn's popular Sunday chicken suppers. Mendel's brick block is seen on the north side of Main Street.

circa **1925  Maplewood Inn** - Harley Mosher changed the name of the Allen Inn to Maplewood Inn when he purchased it in 1922. In 1925 he enclosed the west porch as additional dining room space.

circa **1925  Maplewood Inn** - Looking west from Richmond Avenue, the Maplewood Inn is on the left.  Good use was made of horse drawn wagons and carriages long after automobiles were available.  Notice the electric streetlight.

circa **1939  Maplewood Inn**  -  The Inn sat empty for a time in the late 1930s until the Ontario Bible Conference purchased it in1940 to house attendees at their annual summer conferences.

circa **1943  Maplewood Lodge**  -  In 1940 the Ontario Bible Conference purchased Maplewood Inn, changing its name to Maplewood Lodge.  What had started out as Barrus House in 1875, served its final purpose as lodging for conference visitors.  The last conference at Fair Haven was held in the summer of 1946.

In 1952 the fixtures were sold and the structure was dismantled.  The village of Fair Haven purchased the property for a park and today this park is the center of many activities and events.

OSWEGO PALLADIUM-TIMES
THURSDAY, MAY 22, 1952

FAIR HAVEN

Maplewood Lodge
Sold, Strusture
To Be Torn Down

More Modern Building Will Be
Erected Later On Fair
Haven Site

FAIR HAVEN — Maplewood Lodge, better known as the Fair Haven hotel, has been purchased by Michael Lombardo and will be torn down soon.  Eventually a more modern building will be erected. This hotel, known first as the Barrus House, was built about 80 years ago. It has had many owners and occupants, the last owner being Mr. Stolp. Some of the previous owners and occupants have been: Giles Barrus and his sons. Oscar and Burt; J. N. Russell. George Chappell, J. N. Dietel, Herbert Lindsley, Mr. Strong, N. Woodruff. Charles VanHorn. H. C. Mosher, Ontario Bible Conference. Davis Brothers Mr. Swartz. Burt Ford and Wi Allen.

circa **1958** **Fair Haven Garage** - This building originally served as the carriage house for the Hotel Dietel nest door and was located behind the hotel facing Richmond Avenue. It was moved to face Main Street after becoming an automobile garage.

### Roy Maynard

In 1913 Roy received the Carnegie Medal for Heroism after jumping into the Oswego River to rescue a fellow worker from drowning.

In 1918 he opened the Fair Haven garage and ran it for more than sixty years. Generations of Fair Haven kids remember him fixing their bicycles. A memorial in the park where his garage stood lists some of his many contributions to the community.

**August 10, 1973
Fair Haven Garage**

Raymond T. Sant,
Heather Vickers,
Roy Maynard and
Harley Hendricks on
the occasion of Roy's
86th birthday.

Heather sits on what
was notoriously
known as the
*Loafers and Liars Bench*.

circa **1958 Loafers and Liars Club** - The club was headquartered at Roy Maynard's garage and was well known for propagating humorous tall tales. Walter Phillips, Raymond T. Sant, Carlton Brown, Lawrence Turner and Roy Maynard were charter members.

circa **1925 Fair Haven Garage** - Roy Maynard, in his overalls at left, operated this garage for more than sixty years. He filled an early need in Fair Haven for early automobile owners.

The home on the right, beyond the trees, at Fancher Avenue was built for Fayette Phillips in 1882 when he was partner in the Robinson & Phillips store located across Main Street.

**1958 Phillips House** - Fair Haven's library books were once kept at this residence when the librarian lived here. William and Walter Phillips gave the house to village of Fair Haven in 1958 to be used as a permanent public library.

## 1926  MacArthur House

The house on the left sits on the south west corner of Main Street at Fancher Avenue.  It was built shortly after the *Cottage Farm* lots were sold, about 1875. The porch was added in 1885 and the rear section was added in 1905.

## circa 1926  Griggs House

This house was built about 1875 for John McCrea.  It has now been in the Griggs family for several decades.

ONE POUND        NET WEIGH

OUR

GOLD COIN

BRAND

COFFEE

STEEL CUT

We recommend our "Gold Coin" Brand of Coffee.  It has been carefully selected then cleaned and roasted by modern machinery and is guaranteed to be pure and good

PACKED EXPRESSLY FOR

GRIGGS & McARTHUR,

PHONE 3 Y 5

FAIR HAVEN, N. Y.

When Dr. Leon Griggs lived here in 1926 his office was on the west side.

Veterans of the Union Army who fought in The War of the Rebellion (the Civil War) formed local groups known as **The GAR** (Grand Army of the Republic) which met regularly throughout their lives.

**Members of The GAR, the last eight Civil War veterans in Sterling**
back row **D. R. Garner, Henry Brace, Samuel Brown,
William Butler, Alexander Campbell**
seated **Frederick Turner, Charles Howland, Miles Dakin**

# Friends & Neighbors

## Forefathers, Mothers and Others

**The Gang Pauses For A Photo On Main Street**

John McGibbon, Herb McGibbon, Seward W.,
George Fields, unknown child, Howard Blanchard

**Sterling and Oswego men during exercises at Fair Haven
during the Spanish American War**

**Burt Sampson**
Spanish American War

**Lawrence M. Turner**
The Great War

**World War I Servicemen** - These soldiers gathered at Fair Haven before shipping out to fight *The Great War*.

Before World War II we had no need to number the wars. It was thought that *The Great War* would prove to be the one and only world war.

**1918 Leon Griggs, March Phillips, Lawrence Turner**
The Great War

**Gene Stevenson**

**Bob Hilton**

**Raymond Forsythe**

World War II

**1945 World War II Servicemen**

back row Al Smith, Wesley Bonner, Jack Harrison, Chuck Wilkinson, Gene Stevenson, William Baggs, Bob Bond
front row Theodor Folts, Bob Hilton, Frank Segar, Bill Card

This photograph was taken in front of Food Haven on the north east corner of Main and Lake Streets.

**Dwight Grant**
World War II

**Freida** and **George Sheldon**
1953

Veterans **Osgar Elmer, Dr. Leon Griggs** and **Leland Demarest**
50 years after The Great WarI

Garett Van Fleet

Isaac Turner

Oscar Miller

Elizabeth Miller

**M. C. Turner** and **Friend**

unknown,
unknown and **David King**

Seth Turner, Jr.

Roy Bloomingdale

Christian and Sarah Hunting Sant

John Mc Elveney

Leonard Sant, Allen Sant
and Charles H. Sant

110

William Beyer

Elizabeth Smith Beyer

Clarisa Beyer Clark
"Aunt Tilly"

George I. Post

Martha Mitton Cochrane, George Cochrane, William Cochrane,
Raymond Cochrane, Belle Cochrane, James Cochrane

William "Brannikey"
McFadden

Will Grant

Lavinia Mitton Schuyler

Benjamin Franklyn Hill
and Mary Louise Beyer Hill

Elizabeth Hill Carris

Gladys Louise Hill

1914

Carrie McFadden

Velma Moore

Gladys Hill

Olive Grant

Cora Carter

Madeline Vine

circa **1912** **Fair Haven Suffrage Meeting** - New York State allowed women to vote in 1918. In 1920 the 19th Amendment was passed forcing all states to allow women the right to vote. Today, millions of women in other parts of the world are still waiting for this right.

1 Ada Turner
2 or 3 Mrs John Phillips
4 Bessie Wyman Howell
5 Mae Bennett
6 Effie Truman
7 Iva Phillips Vought
8 Liela Phillips
9 _____
10 Irma Vought
11 Mayme Van Fleet Bennett
12 Minnie Bradley
13 Mrs. Hewett
14 Mrs. M. C. Wells Turner
15 _____
16 _____
17 Maude Snyder

18 Eva Beast
19 Mrs. Baily
20 Clara Philips
21 Mrs. Smith
23 Mrs. Beyer?
24 Sally Ann Cooper
25 Mrs. Fred Turner
26 Mary "Mame" Beyer Hill
27 Dora Bradley Brown
28 Dora Moore
29 Ella Hilton
30 Minnie Wright
31 Mrs. Turner
32 _____
33 _____

Mary Grant Longley

Beulah Grant Leonard

Hazel McFadden and
Arlene Turner

Carrie, Clarinda and Hazel
McFadden

1914
**The Longley Family**

Harold, Colby

Merle, Earnest,
     Grace, Leon

Wilbur, Gordon

**Dr. Ira J.** and **Lucy Rogers Hill**

**Bob Hill**,
Fair Haven Mayor,
holding an ice pick used in
harvesting ice from the bay

Liva P. Church

circa **1885  Fair Haven Band** - Many groups performed around Fair Haven early on. Liva P. Church officially organized the Fair Haven Band in the 1880s. Other original members where A. M. Beyer, Fred Dominy, A. L. Hayward, George Jackson, W. McEachron, James McFarland, Burton McIntyre, Perry McLaughlin, H. C. Pickett, W. B. Reed, F. P. Simpkins and A. L. Toledo.

**September 20, 1923  Fair Haven Citizens Band**

**George E. Rich**
Conductor of the Fair Haven
Band for 25 years

**Milo Vagge**

**1925 Fair Haven Citizens Band** - (back row) George E. Rich, Harry Longley, Robert Monaghan, Charles N. Brown, Mr. Stewart, Ralph Brown, M. D. Russell, Raymond Russell, Sela Travis, Foster Smith, Clay Coppernoll, Lyle Smith, John Phillips, Charles Wright. (seated) Fred Brace, Liva P. Church, Carlton Brown, Ralph Roy, James Wright, Dwight Grant, John McDougall, Arthur Hill, Thurston Smith, Roy Maynard.

### 1904 Fair Haven Baseball Team

Some folks complained that team members should be local boys, saying that bringing in players from other areas was unfair. What would they think of today's teams trading players and entire teams moving to new cities?

back row unknown pitcher from Oswego, Bill Bradley, Thomas Hunter, Fred Hopkins (Cato), Zip Northrup (Cato), unknown catcher from Oswego center attorney, Henry F. Millard front row Joe DeShane, Mr. Bowdish, Harry Jackson, Howard Turner

BASEBALL
Three Games
FAIR HAVEN,
New York
PLEASE DISPLAY

unknown, **Ann Parsons, Floyd Parsons** and **David Parsons**

circa **1904  Paul & Cassius Wilkinson**  -  Paul later operated
*Hill Top Dairy* just south of Fair Haven on Shortcut Road.

## North Fair Haven School

Marie Bennett Phillips and her students at the North Fair Haven schoolhouse.

## Miss Ball's Class

Can you fill in any of the missing names?

Charles Van Patten  Thelma Vright  Doris Bailey  Loretta Eastman
___ Hollenbeck  Donald McKnight  Ethel Sant
Mildred Harris  Ruby Carter  Robert Howell
Marjorie Scott  Florence Turner  Ruby Wall
George Pettit  Mae Harris  Cecil Grummons  Bernice Griggs
Floyd Vine  Floyd Hollenbeck  ___  ___  Fred Simmons
                                    Ernie Breeze  Wm. Bailey
                                                Miss Ball

back row **George Green, George Bailey, Ruben Stevenson, Lawrence Fuller, Harry Humphrey, Jay Frost** front row **Harold LaDue, Walter Parsons, Mary Maynard, Eileen Hickey, Dorothy Baggs, Jean Card, Lawrence Schaffer, Erwin Fineout**

1940
Ward Lyons and Willis Powell

circa **1923** **Nellie Marvin** and the Harris sisters, **Dorothy, Harriet** and **Marion**

**Sarah Harrison**

**Will Baggs**

Oscar Vought

Mit Russel

Dorothy Ingersoll

Frank Eldredge

**1919  Sant House**  -   In front of the Sant House on Victory Street.
back row Florence Scott, Leora Scott, Minerva Sant
front row Marie Scott, Lucille Scott, Dorothy Scott

**Raymond T.** and
**Mabelle Spafford Sant**

Author of books on
Fair Haven and
Sterling history, Ray
Sant served as the
Superintendent of
Schools for Cayuga
County and was
instrumental in the
creation of the first
centralized school in
New York State.

The Three Minervas
**Minerva Sant Sweeting,
Minerva Jane Sant and
Minerva Sant Austin**

**Minerva Jane Sant Brockman**

**Walter Phillips**

**Wells Bennett**

circa **1927** **Reforestation Team**

back row Clarence Fineout, Larry Galloway, Richard Woodruff, John Holbert, Kenneth Bailey, Addison Cotell, Reuben Stevenson.

middle row Russell Tanner, Marjorie Hilton Stevenson, Flora Wilkinson, Freda Hilton, Dorothy Scott, Beth Woodruff.

front row Dwight Grant, unknown, John Parsons, Richard Farnsworth, George Bailey.

By 1850 most of Sterling's nearly unbroken virgin forest had been cleared. Most of the trees we have today are managed second growth and would not have come back as quickly or densely on their own.

**Robert Downey**

Carroll Stark, Lydia Stark, William Stark, Caroline Stark, Fay Stark

Mr. & Mrs. Charles Wilde and Mr. & Mrs. Wall Reed

**1942 The Spaffords** -  Carrie, Virtue, Bud, Emma and Etta

**1950 Double Cousins** -  These cousins share ancestors on both sides of their families. standings Flora Hill, Will Brooks, Elmer Carris, Frank Ditgen seated Emma McEachron, J. S. Brooks, Ann Justus

## Wilford W. Green

Wilford was a descendent of Revolutionary War general, Nicholas Herkimer. Will spent part of his childhood at the Herkimer Home.

In this photograph he holds a door latch from the house that family members had kept as an heirloom. An avid historian, when the homestead became a state park Will returned the latch and key to the home.

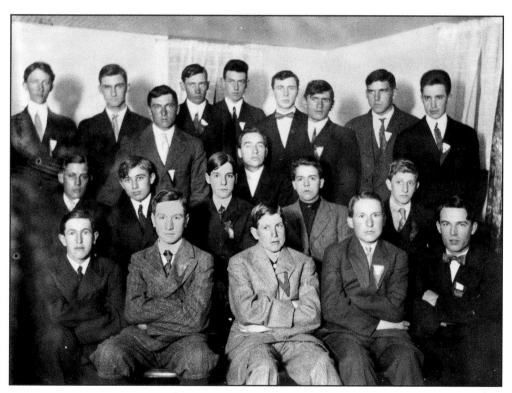

*Who Do* **Class** - Members of Reverend John Sharpe's Presbyterian "Who Do" class back row Ludo McCrea, Floyd Schouten, Roy Carter, Eben Andrews, John Forscutt, Leon Byer, Floyd Farnsworth, Henry Carter, Walter Phillips middle row Leonard Lyon, Clifton Pettit, Lawrence Turner, Reverend Sharpe, Walter Collins, Levi King front row Leon Sampson, Harry Smith, Kenneth Bradley, Carl Topping, Harry Brown

**1937 McIntyre Brothers - Elwyn, Marshall, George** and **Clarence**

circa **1935 The Cool Guys** - Martin Burtless, Seward Smith, Lyman Smith and Russell Grant in front of the post office.

# Fair Haven Mysteries

6

## What Do You Know?

**Mystery One** - Do you know where this house was located?
Do you recognize any of the members of this family?

# Fair Haven Mysteries

What are the clues in these photographs that reveal where they might have been taken? Perhaps you recognize something in the background that provides a clue to the where it is or maybe you know someone you think might remember one of these places.

In most cases the photographs are completely unmarked and I am trying to find out where the house or building was/is located. It may have been somewhere in Sterling or nearby in Wayne County or Oswego County. Please take a look and see if any of these questions jog your memory.

You can email, call, write to me or go online and add your comment about the image at: www.OurHistoricalSociety.Org

Rob Kolsters
Post Office Box 4319
Burbank, California 91503

818-763-5800

RKolsters@DocumentedResearch.Org

www.OurHistoricalSociety.Org

**Mystery Two**

Do you know where this cottage was/is?

**Mystery Three** - Do you have a photograph of the *octagon house* that once stood on the west side of the bay? Perhaps you have a photograph taken from a boat or from the west bar that shows it in the background.

**Mystery Four** - Notice the church steeple at center and the house with a cuppola to the right. Is this Little Sodus Bay or another bay?

**Mystery Five** - Is there a house in Sterling that still has log cabin walls or beams as part of its original structure? Where was the last log cabin in Sterling?

**Mystery Six** - Where was the first Little Sodus Post Office located when Seth Turner was postmaster in 1828?

**Mystery Seven** - This postcard was mailed on April 15, 1907 from the Fair Haven post office. Do you recognize this cottage? Where was/is it?

**Mystery Eight** - Notice the view on the left and the three houses in the background on the right. Do you know where this house was/is located?

**Mystery Nine** - Notice the view on the right and the arbor. Do you know where this cottage was/is located?

**Mystery Ten**

Do you know where this house was/is located?

Could this be the home of George Moak on South Fancher Avenue?

Where did George live?

**Mystery Eleven**- Where was/is this house located? Who lived here?

**Mystery Twelve** - This camp was known as "Dunworkin." Where was/is it?

**Mystery Thirteen** - Notice the "Hotel" sign over the front porch and the house next door on the left. Do you know where this house was/is located?

# Preservation

7

## See What You Have

**Restoring Image Contrast** - Faded images can be brought back to life. Don't discard them.

### Rescuing Images of Fair Haven

This chapter attempts to *show* some of the many reasons why all images and documents are valuable and should be saved. Faded or damaged images can be restored. Unidentified people and places can be researched and compared with other photographs. Methods of preservation and restoration continually improve.

**Building Locations** - All of the buildings in this photograph are now gone. When the photographer snapped this photo of ball practice the relative locations of the Fair Haven railroad depot and the apple dryer were recorded.

### House in Background

If someone had discarded this photograph of paving work on Main Street because they do not know the names of these men, we would have lost a valuable example of one of Fair Haven's early houses. In the background we see the home of Darius S. Cole as it appeared before it was remodeled. This home may have been built as early as 1828.

We would have also lost this example of how road work was done. One day we may find other photographs of these men that will help to identify them.

## Don't Throw History Away

It takes many people to hand down historical documents decade after decade. It only takes one person to bring an end to the diligent effort of so many others. Every photograph someone might think of discarding is of value in some way. If you have photographs, newspapers or other items you do not want, receive a tax write-off by donating them to the Sterling Historical Society.

**Magnification** - Both, the film you put in the camera and the paper a photograph is "printed" on, are coated with chemicals that respond to light on a microscopic level. A real photograph is not "printed," it is "developed." The photographic process is an organic reaction of molecules which captures much more detail than today's digital images.

For example if you look closely at an image in a magazine, the human eye can see the tiny dots that make up the picture on the page. You can not "blow up" this image because it is created though a "printing" processes and not "developed" though a photographic process.

A real photograph contains detail the human eye can not see. This is why computer scanners that are more sensitive than the human eye can reveal these details for us.

## Microfilm

This photograph of the interior of the Dietel Hardware Store appeared in the newspaper. This is how the image appears on the microfilm version.

The location of the original photograph is unknown.

## Newspaper

This version was scanned from the original newspaper.

## Computer Restoration

This is the same scanned image ② from the newspaper after computer restoration.

**Original Newspapers** - Original copies of newspapers should be preserved, even if copies are available on microfilm. Microfilm is an old technology that does not compare in quality to real documents. The film is often over exposed by the operator. Many pages are entirely unreadable or missing.

**Lost Forever** - When the Old Brutus Historical Society loaned some of its newspapers to a reputable institution to be put on microfilm, no one informed them that their papers would not be returned. The original papers were destroyed. Many organizations that do microfilming and scanning don't understand that backup copies are a necessary precaution, but cannot compare to original documents. This is only one of the reasons it is important that we save all issues that turn up.

This is an example of a newspaper page on microfilm.
It is mostly unreadable and no original copy of this issue is known to exist.

**Missing Pages** - On the right is an example of a page from The Fair Haven Register on microfilm. Clippings had already been cut from it before it was microfilmed. Entire pages are missing from some issues.

**Missing Issues** - Microfilm reels marked as containing sequential issues over a span of years, sometimes contain less than half of the issues printed during the time span indicated.

The microfilm label reading "Fair Haven Register 1890 to 1895" creates the illusion that someone has already preserved a complete set of these issues. In reality this film role contain only *some* of the issues printed during these years.

## Making Copies

Every year well preserved items are lost to flood, fire, hurricane, tornado and other disasters. It is well known that the best way to ensure that ephemera survives into the future is to make as many copies as possible and store them in different places. This was one of the concepts behind microfilm.

Leviticus

Like the many handwritten copies of ancient books of the bible buried in jars and caves, only a few copies of our documents may survive the journey through time. However, as with these, enough copies can be made so that some will be found.

Today we can scan and print high quality copies of documents & photographs and easily store digital backup copies in each place future researchers may look.

With these preservation tools available to us, the loss of an original document that was never copied is a great and unnecessary loss.

## Forensic History

New technologies are continually being invented that will allow us to do even more with old images we thought were unrecoverable.

For example, there is now a computer program that will examine a license plate that is too blurry to read and determine the only set of characters that could create the same blurry shape.

## How Contrast Works

When a photograph fades, all areas usually fade the same amount. A scanner can detect over a million different shades of gray the human eye cannot distinguish.

Computer software can then reassign each shade of gray to a broader scope of black to white. The darkest gray area is changed to black and the lightest area is changed to white. The shades of gray in between are then adjusted in similar amounts to restore the full range of contrast.

This is a simplified explanation of the basic principle to show why this is possible. Faded color images work the same way by making each color darker and lighter.

The person making these adjustments on the computer does not "invent" anything that is not really present in the faded photograph.

## Digital Scanning

In the preservation of photographic images, scanners should be set to the highest optical resolution available. Details revealed by the scanner that we can not see can be invaluable in identifying, people, places and events.

Magnifying a calendar on the wall can reveal the year a photograph was taken. April 1 falls on a Wednesday about once every seven years.

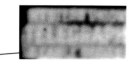

**Western Union TELEGRAPH**

Scanning at a higher resolution is like using a magnifying glass to look at a photograph.

A low resolution scanned image may look okay on the screen, but not print well and it cannot be enlarged.

Higher resolution scanning allows for enlarging areas of the image.

**Information** - One of the values of restoring photographs is to read text that can help reveal the historical information such as the date the photograph and other comparable photographs were taken. This image gives us a feel for how wide Main Street was for the first 100 years. The photographer is standing in

the shadow of the Robinson & Phillips store, built in 1881. In the background on the left, the buildings on Richmond Avenue have not yet been built. The shadows show it is afternoon & the leaves on the trees suggest it is early spring.

Correcting the contrast shows us that this is the Hotel Dietel, though the stairs once extending along the full length of the front porch have been

replaced with a railing
and the second floor railing
replaced in the same style.

## Street Lamp

Fair Haven's first street lamps were oil burning lanterns with just enough oil to last into the wee hours.

**Spot Sits with Walter and Carl Phillips**

The hitching post has a convenient ring at the top through which you can tether your horse.

**4th of July Parade** - The annual Fair Haven 4th of July parade has been going on for longer than anyone can remember. People from far and wide enjoy the parade on Main Street and the fireworks on the bay. Do you have any old photo of parade days?

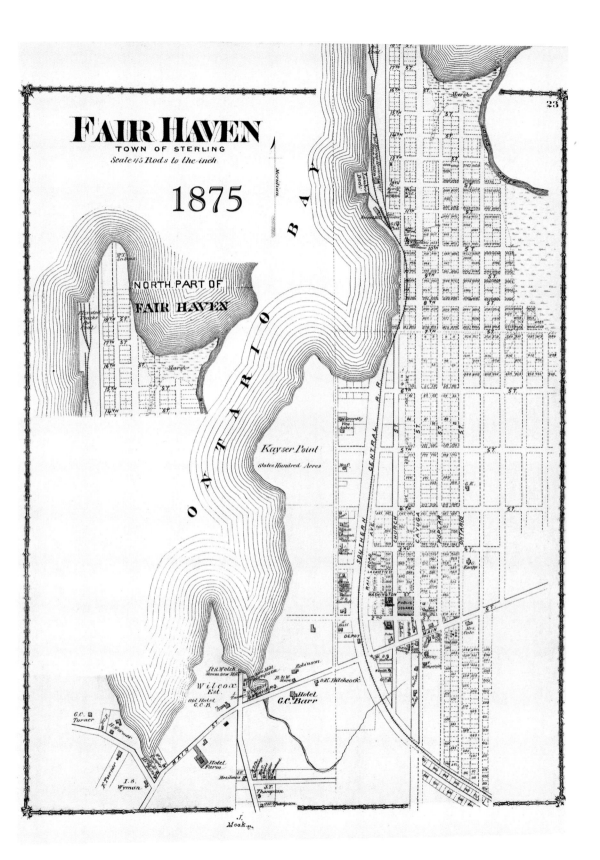

# FAIR HAVEN

## TOWN OF STERLING

*Scale 45 Rods to the inch*

# 1875

NORTH PART OF
**FAIR HAVEN**

O N T A R I O   B A Y

Kayser Point
*States Hundred Acres*

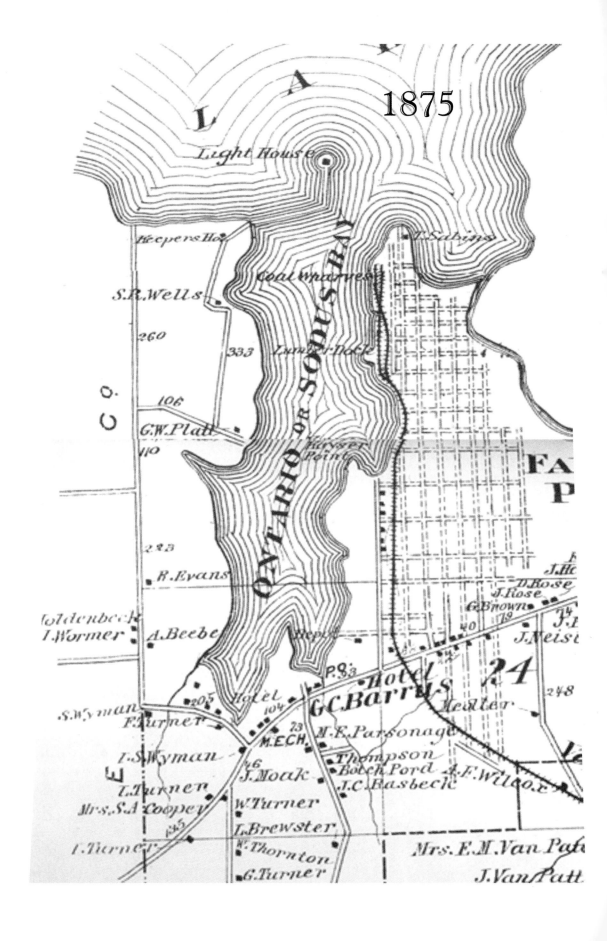

1875

L A

Light House

Keepers Ho.

S.R.Wells

260

333

106

G.W.Platt

110

Coal wharves

Lumber Dock

ONTARIO or SODUS BAY

T.Sabins

FA
P

Keyser
Point

223

R.Evans

Oldenbeck
I.Wormer

A.Beebe

Depot

Co.

J.H.
D.Rose
J.Rose
G.Brown

40

J.Neise

J.
248

205

S.Wyman

F.Turner

Hotel
104

P.O.

23

M.ECH.

Hotel
G.C.Barry's

M.E.Parsonage

Heisler

24

I.S.Wyman

L.Turner

Mrs.S.A.Cooper
285

J.Moak

W.Turner

L.Brewster

Thompson
Botch Ford
J.C.Basbeck

J.F.Willco.

I.Turner

W.Thornton
G.Turner

Mrs.E.M.Van Pat
J.VanPatt.

# Index

**Charles H. Sweeting** - Author of *200 Years of Cayuga County, NY Postal History* and *Oswego County, NY Postal History*, Charlie loved Fair Haven so much that he knew he must also write a book about the Village. As a child, he spent many weekends at the home of his grandparents, Charlie and Belle McElveney Sant, on Victory Street. As a teenager, he bicycled from Auburn to Fair Haven whenever weather allowed.

Charlie's ancestors were among the first to arrive at Fair Haven in the early 1800s. Many members of the Sant family have remained in or near the Village, or have spent their summers here, so Fair Haven is a family place.

Unfortunately, Charlie's health did not allow him to see this published version of the book. But, he enjoyed creating it and knew what it would mean to those who love Fair Haven.

**Robert J. Kolsters** - Rob's great-great-grandparents, William and Mercy Firth Mitton, came to Fair Haven in the mid 1800s. His grandfather left him a treasure of family stories and genealogical information that pointed him toward Little Sodus Bay, where he immediately fell under Fair Haven's spell. He has spent several years traveling from Fair Haven to archives around the country transcribing, photo-copying and scanning all things Fair Haven.

Rob published the *Swamp Angel* (resurrecting the name of Fair Haven's first newspaper) for two years, recounting stories from Sterling's history. His interests so impressed the Sterling Historical Society they deputized him *Historian-At-Large*.

Seeing the variety of photographs scattered about in many collections he recognized the need to bring them together as a book for Sterling and Fair Haven. When Charlie suggested that they collaborate on such a book, Rob jumped at the opportunity to work with him.

**Charlie Sweeting** with **Betsy** and their twin
grandchildren, **Charles** and **Ashley Kuczawa**
on the front steps of the Sant house
on Victory Street.

There is nothing Charlie loved more than
getting out to "Grandma's" house to
play ... and he never loved it more than
on the 4th of July Parade days with
his grand kids ... This was taken the
summer after his heart transplant.